AT HOME ON THE EARTH

By Jim Bruchac and Joseph Bruchac III

Modern Curriculum Press
Parsippany, New Jersey

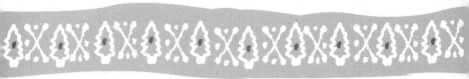

Credits

Photos: All photos © Pearson Learning unless otherwise noted.
Front cover: Rick Gargiulo. Title page: Joseph Bruchac. 5: NASA. 6: David
Muench/Corbis. 7: Nick Hawkes/Ecoscene/Corbis. 9: Rick Gargiulo. 10: Library of
Congress. 11: James Bruchac. 13: North Wind Picture Archives. 16: James Bruchac.
17: U.S. Department of Agriculture. 19: Lonny Kalfus/Stone. 20, 22, 23, 25, 26: James
Bruchac. 27: Joseph Bruchac. 28, 29, 30, 31, 32, 33: James Bruchac. 34: Courtesy of
The Saratogian. 35, 36: James Bruchac. 38: Lee Cates/PhotoDisc, Inc. 39: *l.* Pat
O'Hara/Corbis; *r.* Scott T. Smith/Corbis. 41: David A. Northcott/Corbis. 42: James
Bruchac. 43: Rick Gargiulo. 44: James Bruchac. 45: Joseph Bruchac. 46: Justin
Kennick. 47: Linda Morey.

Illustrations: 8: Mapping Specialists

Cover and book design by Lisa Ann Arcuri

Modern Curriculum Press

An imprint of Pearson Learning
299 Jefferson Road, P.O. Box 480
Parsippany, NJ 07054–0480

www.pearsonlearning.com

1-800-321-3106

ISBN 0-7652-2167-5

2 3 4 5 6 7 8 9 10 11   MA   07 06 05 04 03 02 01

Contents

In memory of my grandmother,
Marion Flora Bowman Bruchac,
for her laughter and friendship

Chapter 1

Sharing the Earth

Traveling through the darkness of space is a bright, colorful planet we call Earth. Some people who have seen Earth from space have described it as looking like a blue, green, and brown marble with swirls of white.

A photograph of Earth, taken from outer space

In a meadow and elsewhere, all living things depend on plants.

Earth is the only home we know. It is also the home we share with thousands of plants and animals of all kinds. All the living things on the earth are connected. We need each other to survive.

Plants are especially important. They help clean the air by taking in carbon dioxide and giving off oxygen. They help make the ground rich and fertile. Plants hold down the soil so that it doesn't wash or blow away. They also provide food and shelter for many other living things. Without plants, animals and people could not live.

Earth's plants and animals also need clean air and water to stay healthy. More and more people are realizing that these necessary things are not as easy to find as they used to be. In many places the air and water are dirty, and plants no longer grow. In many places the number of animals has decreased. Some kinds of plants and animals have disappeared from the earth forever. People are beginning to see how important it is to take care of our home.

Taking care of a whole planet is not easy. First, you have to learn all about the land and the plants and animals that live on it. People can begin to understand how all living things are connected by working with and living close to the land. This understanding helps people to respect and want to protect the earth.

Pollution hurts the water and all the living things that depend on water.

There is a place where people of all ages can go to learn about the earth and its plants and animals. This place is in Greenfield Center, New York, in the foothills of the Adirondack Mountains. It is called the Ndakinna (ihn-DAH-kih-nah) Education Center and Nature Preserve.

Run by members of the Bruchac family, the Center offers many programs. Visitors can learn how to travel through the woods without getting lost. They can learn how to find edible plants and safe drinking water. All of the programs are based on traditional Native American ways.

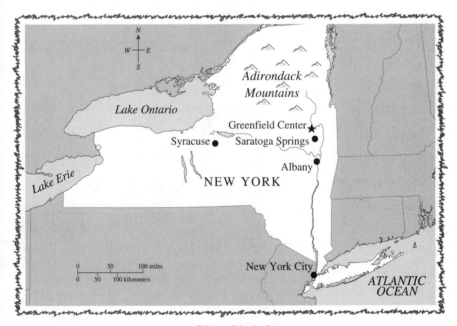

Map of New York State

Hello, my name is Jim Bruchac, and I am going to tell you about this wonderful place. The Ndakinna Education Center and Nature Preserve is a place that I know well, not only because I am one of the founders. It is a place my family has called home for over a hundred years. Both the teachings and the history of my family are deeply rooted in this land.

Jim Bruchac

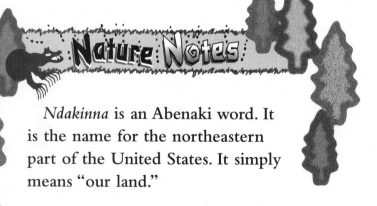

Nature Notes

Ndakinna is an Abenaki word. It is the name for the northeastern part of the United States. It simply means "our land."

Chapter 2

The First People

The first people who lived on the land I now call my home and in nearby Saratoga Springs were Native Americans. They included the Mahicans (mah HEE kunz). These people were part of a larger group called Algonquins (ahl GAHNG kee unz). The Algonquins shared a similar culture and spoke variations of the same language. Many people today believe that the Mahicans lived in this area for over 10,000 years.

About a thousand years ago, another group of people called the Iroquois (IHR uh kwoi) moved into this area from the west. These people later became known as the Mohawks.

Mohawk Chief Joseph Brant

A wigwam

Mahicans and Mohawks had a strong respect for the land. Everything they used came from the forest. They did not take anything from the land that they did not need. Their clothing and tools were made from the animals they hunted for food. They also grew crops such as corn, beans, pumpkins, sunflowers, and squash. In fact, Native American people were the first to develop these crops.

The people made houses that were rounded on the top and covered with tree bark. They called their homes *wigwams* or *wigomak*. The word *wigwam* means "house" in the Algonquin language. Larger wigwams are sometimes called longhouses. Several families could live in a longhouse.

Both Algonquin and Iroquois people thought of the area surrounding Saratoga Springs as sacred or spiritual. This was because of the mineral springs that many people believed were healing waters. It was considered an area of peace to be shared by all.

The first European to visit the area was an Englishman named Sir William Johnson. Sir William first traded with the Mohawks during the late 1700s. He later became the Superintendent of Indian Affairs for New York State. Sir William also became a friend of the Mohawks. They called him *Warrahiyagey* (WAH-rahg-ee-YAH-gay). This name meant "The One Who Does Much Honest Business With Us."

Sir William found out for himself how wonderful the mineral springs were when he became sick. His Mohawk friends brought him to bathe in the springs and drink the mineral water. Afterward, Sir William said he felt much better.

Soon after Sir William visited the area, other Europeans came and settled there. English colonists bought some of the Mohawk's land. The place where the Ndakinna Center now stands was a part of the land the colonists bought.

The first European settlers were farmers. In some ways the land was very different from what they had been used to in Europe. Many of the animals and plants were new. The weather was also different.

Painting of English colonists living on the land in New York

Once they understood the land better, the settlers lived as the Native Americans had lived. The land provided them with everything they needed for food, shelter, and clothing.

Sheep need the land to graze. Then they can
provide people with wool.

In their gardens the English farmers grew corn,
beans, and squash, just as the Mohawks had done.
They hunted for game such as deer and rabbits in
the forests. They also raised cows, pigs, chickens,
geese, and sheep for wool to make clothing. They
planted hay and oats to feed their animals. They
used the same plants Indians used for medicine
when they were sick. They also grew other plants
they had brought from England.

Unlike the Mohawks, the settlers cleared away much of the forest to plant their crops and make their homes. They built their houses from whole trees that they cut. They also cut down many trees for firewood for heat and cooking. More trees were cut down as more people moved into the area. Within the next two centuries, most of the area's forests were gone.

Nature Notes

The different tribes of the Iroquois people who lived in New York State had a well-organized government. The tribes met and made their laws together.

Chapter

3

Family Ties

By the 1800s most of the Greenfield Center land was owned by the Dunham family. The Dunhams were my great-great-grandparents. They bought the land for farming and for wood cutting in the forest areas that were left.

While living there, they built a sawmill and a cider mill. A sawmill is a place where logs are cut to make boards for building. A cider mill is where apples are pressed and turned into juice.

My great-great-grandparents with my
great-grandmother Marion Edna Dunham

Farmers used horses to plow a field.

In the early 1900s, each of the Dunham children were given a farm and some land. This is how my great-grandparents, Marion Dunham Bowman and Jesse Bowman, became the owners of about 100 acres where my home is now.

Jesse Bowman's family were Abenaki (ah ben AH kee). These people were eastern cousins of the Mahicans. Jesse had a strong love for nature like his Native American ancestors. One of his favorite things to do was walk in the woods.

Great-Grampa Jesse and his wife learned to respect the land as they worked hard to farm it. Long ago, farmers did not have tractors. Just as other farmers did, my great-grandparents used horses to pull a plow. The plow broke up the ground so crops could be planted.

When horses grew old in those days, many farmers would sell them to factories. The factories would make dog food from the meat and also glue from the horse bones and hide. Great-Grampa Jesse loved his old horses too much to do that. He kept them. When an old horse finally died, he buried it in one of the farm fields. This is the same field where we do outdoor education programs today.

Besides farming, Great-Grampa Jesse and his wife, Marion, ran a little general store near their home and farm. They called it Bowman's Store. A general store is a store that sells almost everything people might need. This includes food, tools, and clothing.

My great-grandparents had only one child. Her name was Marion Flora Bowman. She was my grandmother. In 1940, Marion Flora married Joseph Bruchac, Jr. Shortly after their wedding, my great-grandparents gave the young couple most of the land they had gotten from their parents. My great-grandparents kept two acres and Bowman's Store.

My Grampa Joe sold a few acres to friends and family. Most of the land stayed intact. He too had a strong love for the land. He had hunted and fished there since he was a small boy. In the 1930s, there was a Great Depression. People had no jobs and little to eat. My grandfather hunted and trapped to provide food for his parents and his brothers and sisters.

My grandfather allowed most of the old forest on his land to grow back. He also put up several new buildings. These new buildings, along with the old barns, became his Adirondack Taxidermy Studio. A taxidermist is someone who preserves the heads or bodies of animals that have been hunted. You can see such preserved and mounted animals in many museums. My grandfather was such a good taxidermist that he was named to the Taxidermist Hall of Fame.

The Bruchac Family Tree

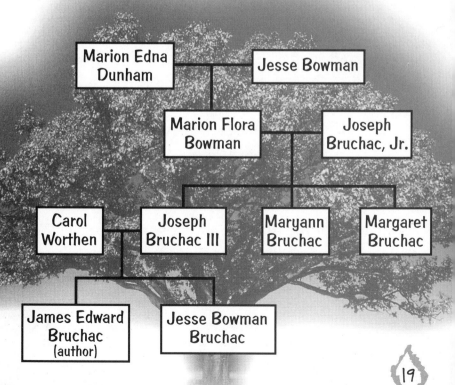

My grandparents had three children, two girls and a boy. They grew up playing in the Bruchac forest. The oldest child, Joseph Bruchac III, is my father.

When my father grew up, he married my mother, Carol. In 1968, I was born. Soon after my birth, my parents moved in with my Great-Grampa Jesse.

Next to Bowman's Store there was also an old gas station. The little store no longer had much business. My family knew how much it meant to my great-grandfather, so they kept the store open until Great-Grampa Jesse died in 1970. My parents stayed in the house. In 1972 my brother, Jesse, was born.

Bowman's Store and
Great-Grampa Jesse's house

Like our relatives before us, my brother and I spent many of our waking hours exploring the Bruchac forest. Sometimes our dad would come along. He showed us many of the plants, trees, and animals that lived there. He taught us to be quiet in the forest. We learned how to listen, and to use our eyes just as my father's grandfather had taught him to do.

Great-Grampa Jesse always had time to spend with my dad when he was a child. Great-Grampa Jesse would point out the tracks of animals or tell him the names of flowers and plants. He taught my father how they could be used as food or medicine. He helped my dad catch his first trout and reminded him to say thank you to the fish for allowing him to catch it. Jesse's love of the forest inspired my dad to seek out and share Native American ways of life when he grew up. Although we didn't realize it at the time, our dad's love of the forest did the same for us.

I always loved sharing the forest with others. My brother and I would play games there with friends. As I got older, the forest was also a good place for me to get away and be by myself. We spent so much time in the Bruchac forest as kids that it became as familiar to us as your living room might be to you.

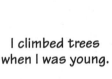

I climbed trees when I was young.

Nature Notes

There is a big old pine tree in the middle of the Bruchac forest. I still love to sit under this tree. One time a deer walked right in front of me. I stayed perfectly still and it didn't even see me.

Chapter 4

Rooted in Tradition

My father, Joseph Bruchac III, was raised by his Abenaki grandfather, Jesse Bowman. There were not many other children around where he grew up. So my father often played by himself in the forest or walked by his Grampa Jesse's side.

My Great-Grampa Jesse with my father, Joe Bruchac III

Although Grampa Jesse talked to my father a lot about animals, nature, and gardening, he never spoke much about his Abenaki roots. This was because he and his family, along with other Native Americans, had been treated badly by other people because they were Indians.

My dad wanted to learn about his people's history. He wanted to hear the stories his grandfather had never told him. When he grew up, he traveled around the country to meet Native American elders.

As he collected the stories and traditions, my dad began to share them with others. This is how my dad became known worldwide as a Native American storyteller. He wrote many articles and poems that have been published in more than 500 magazines. He also wrote more than 80 books of poetry, fiction, and nonfiction.

Most of my dad's books are about Native Americans. Many of them are for children. *Thirteen Moons on Turtle's Back* is a collection of poems. Each poem tells the story of one of the 13 moons during the year. *The First Strawberries* tells the story of why the Cherokee are reminded to be kind to each other when they eat strawberries. *Dog People* is a collection of Abenaki stories about children and dogs.

My father, Joseph Bruchac III, tells a Native American story.

One very popular series is the *Keepers of the Earth* books, coauthored by my dad and naturalist Michael Caduto. These books are used by schools across the country. They combine Native American legends with environmental activities. One of the stories tells why only birds and not turtles travel south for the winter. One of the activities that follows the story is making a model of a migrating bird.

The many teachings about the natural world that we got from our father helped my brother and me to learn respect for the natural world. These teachings included many Native American legends. On winter nights my father would often tell us stories.

One of the oldest Abenaki stories my dad told says that people were originally made of stone. Having stone hearts, they had no respect for the earth. They were monsters who crushed everything they saw. Because of this, the original people were broken into small stones and destroyed. Next, people were made from the ash trees. They had strong roots in the ground. When remembering these roots, the people would always have respect for the earth. So the Abenakis are the children of the ash tree.

Young listeners at the Goshen Center School in Connecticut enjoy my father's stories.

Some of my favorite stories that my dad told were about monsters. My love for those stories led to one of my dad's newest books. I wrote this one with him. It is called *When the Chenoo Howls: Native American Tales of Terror.*

I am hard at work writing another book.

Nature Notes

My dad assists other writers, too. My parents turned the old gas station next to the store into The Greenfield Review Literary Center. Here people learn about poetry and buy books published by The Greenfield Review Press. Many of the books are by Native American writers.

Chapter 5

Teaching Begins

My brother and I became more and more interested in our Native American traditions as we grew older. We were especially interested in wilderness skills. We had a chance to learn more when we met John Stokes in 1985. He is director of the Tracking Project.

The Tracking Project specializes in teaching what John calls the Arts of Life. These arts combine wilderness survival skills with traditional dancing, storytelling, and Native American philosophy. A philosophy is knowledge that helps people understand, describe, and relate to the world around them.

John Stokes is especially good at identifying animal tracks. Here he points to some.

I show children at the center how to make and use traditional tools like the bow drill.

John did more than inspire us. He taught us important new skills such as how to use a bow drill. A bow drill is a fire-starting tool that spins a stick on a wooden base. The friction makes fire. John made all the skills and stories he taught seem cool. Being cool was almost as important to us as our Native American heritage.

John asked my brother Jesse and me to work as assistant instructors for his young men's camp in New Mexico. For the next ten years, at least one of us worked for John every summer. Jesse and I loved how the many skills, stories, and teachings at John's camp helped people gain a greater respect for the earth. While working with the Tracking Project, we learned how to teach these skills. We also gained an even greater appreciation for the many things our own father had taught us.

Grandmother Marion with me on the left and my
brother, Jesse, on the right

In 1986 my grandfather, Joseph Bruchac, Jr., died.
My grandmother, Marion, had no interest in
developing the land. So, although our family still
lived there, the buildings sat empty and unused.
These buildings included my grandfather's old
taxidermy studio.

In 1988, Jesse and I began to offer our own
Native American and wilderness programs on the
Bruchac land. My grandmother thought this was a
great idea. We wanted to help people recognize the
importance of connecting with, respecting, and
protecting the earth for future generations.

Each year we did more programs. Our father helped us. We brought in friends who could also teach wilderness skills. We began working with many schoolchildren as well as adults. We shared Native American legends, or stories from the past. We talked about Native American culture and philosophies. We also taught how to identify plants and trees, animal tracking, and wilderness survival.

Our next step was to bring all these teachings and teachers together under one name. So in 1994, my brother and I formed the Ndakinna Wilderness Project. We chose the Abenaki name *Ndakinna* because it represents where we are from and what we are trying to save.

Children learn wilderness skills from me.

The name *Ndakinna* also reminds people that this part of the earth was first cared for by Native Americans and that it is now meant for all of us to share. We called it a Wilderness Project because our skills and teachings were usually based in the natural world itself, away from the towns and cities. Since we started the Project, we have offered programs to hundreds of adults and children.

These children are playing an awareness game in which one player is blindfolded.

Nature Notes

Besides teaching people at the Ndakinna Center, my brother and I also take our programs traveling. We often visit schools to teach children wilderness skills.

Chapter 6

Forever Wild

My grandmother was inspired by our use of the land. She also wanted to preserve it for the future. So in 1991, my grandmother made a big decision. She had been watching houses and malls being built all around us on land where her husband and her father had hunted. She thought about how many generations of her family had loved these acres of forest, fields, and streams. Someone had told her that there was no way to stop progress. Soon it all would be gone, developed into housing, highways, and parking lots.

The Bruchac land today

My grandmother didn't believe in waiting until the forests, fields, and streams were gone. She placed the Bruchac land in a conservation easement through the Saratoga Land Trust. An easement is a kind of law. It allows someone a certain amount of control over someone else's property. Our conservation easement meant that my grandmother would still own the land, but no one would be able to develop it. Our land was set aside in its natural, undeveloped state for educational use. It would always be there so that people could learn from nature instead of losing it.

Marion Flora Bowman makes front page news.

When the easement was made, an article about it appeared on the front page of a local newspaper. The headline said "Forever Wild" and showed a picture of my grandmother. She would often joke that the title referred to her and the land. "We're both forever wild," she would laugh.

No modern structures can be built on the land. However, many educational exhibits have been created. They include a full-size Native American longhouse, three wigwams, and two lean-tos for camping. There are also several native gardens. Nature trails wind their way through the forest with bridges over streams and swamps. There are also signs to identify many of the trees.

Children on one of the many nature trails at Ndakinna

Children at the center examine plaster casts of animal tracks.

As the number of programs offered on our land grew, my grandmother gave us permission in 1995 to use my grandfather's old taxidermy studio. The studio barns became a perfect home for the newly formed Ndakinna Education Center.

Although my grandmother was in a wheelchair, she still loved to take part in our work whenever she could. She took great joy in seeing so many people enjoy the land she had helped protect.

In 1999, my grandmother died. She left much of the land to my brother, Jesse, and to me. In her honor we renamed the land the Marion Bowman Bruchac Nature Preserve.

Nature Notes

Whenever school groups came, the kids would visit my grandmother in her house. They made her gifts such as bead necklaces, painted pictures, and poems they wrote about the land. She always smiled and said, "Hope you had a good time. Come back again."

Chapter

7
Animals and Plants

The land where I live is special to me because so many different plants and animals make their home here. Many would be familiar to you. Some of them might not be. There are deer, woodchucks, porcupines, wild turkeys, minks, raccoons, fisher cats, coyotes, and red-tailed hawks. There are also different kinds of squirrels and foxes, mice, snowshoe hares, ruffed grouse, and even an occasional bear.

A raccoon feeds at the edge of a pond.

Indian Pipe flowers

Lady's slipper

More than 50 kinds of trees grow on our land. There are white pine, sugar maple, black ash, red and white oak, eastern hemlock, beech, shagbark hickory, red sumac, black cherry, American elm, and birch trees.

If you look closer to the ground, you will find many other plants. Some of the flowers have interesting names. There are dog-tooth plants, trilliums, pink lady's slippers, bloodroot, black-eyed Susans, asters, tiger lilies, bladder campions, and violets. If you looked around the wetland areas, you'd find cattails, joe-pye weeds, speckled alders, and wild grapes. In the somewhat drier surrounding areas, there are ferns, Indian Pipes, mosses, and many types of fungi or mushrooms.

Some of the most interesting plants are those the Native Americans once used for medicines. These include dwarf ginseng, jack-in-the-pulpit, milkweed, May apple, red trillium, and golden thread. These plants would be eaten, used to make teas, or made into salves or creams to help people get better when they were sick. All these plants are still used today by many Native Americans and quite a few other people. In fact, many plants have been used to make modern medicines.

One of our oldest stories tells that long ago the plants saw that humans were sick and suffering. They decided to help. The plants came to people when they were dreaming and told them their secrets. To this day it is said by Native Americans that every plant can be used as a medicine if you know the right way to use it. Learning the right ways to use these plants takes time and training, though. You should never eat anything you find outdoors unless you are sure it is safe. It is also wise to avoid touching strange plants, as many are poisonous to touch as well as to eat.

A plant that I have learned to use is the white pine. If I have a cold or a cough, I make a tea by soaking a handful of this tree's green needles in boiling water. When I drink this tea, it soothes my throat and helps to clear my head.

The Eastern tiger salamander makes its home in Bell Brook.

Two streams wind their way through the property. As a child I loved wading in them. The larger stream is named Bell Brook. Many types of fish live here. Crayfish and frogs can be found, too. They are always watchful so they can escape the hungry raccoons. You'll also see many kinds of salamanders, toads, and snakes. None of the snakes is poisonous.

In one corner of our land is a rare type of fossil rock called cryptozoan. The name *cryptozoan* means "hidden or mysterious animals." Fossils are stones that contain the shapes of animals and plants that died long ago. The fossils look like cabbages, but they are the remains of ancient underwater creatures. These creatures lived millions of years ago in a sea that once covered the land.

Nature Notes

Two animals that visitors might meet at the Ndakinna Center are guests who appear at the wilderness weekend workshops. They are Cheyenne, a female timber wolf, and Koda, a female cougar.

Koda

Chapter 8

Present and Future

If you visited the Ndakinna Education Center and Nature Preserve today, you would see many things. You could start in the Education Center. Here you would find dozens of models of homes showing how Northeastern Native Americans once lived. You would also see over 200 plaster casts of animal tracks. These tracks include wolves and grizzly bears. Many of the casts were made from tracks right here on our land.

I am holding a cast of a bear track. The branch supports are for a new wigwam.

My wife, Jean Bruchac, showing Native American food

You might also want to be a part of one of the many programs we offer. Do you think you could survive in the wilderness? How could you build a fire without matches? How would you build a shelter without a hammer and nails? What would you eat? If you came to an Ndakinna youth program, you would learn many of these skills that you would need to survive in the wilderness. Most important, you would learn how to slow down and become more aware of your surroundings.

You would also hear plenty of Native American legends. Some of these stories are funny, and others are a little scary. They also teach valuable lessons. These lessons include the value of sharing and always giving thanks to and respecting the natural world.

Storytelling time in the longhouse

My Aunt Margaret is also a storyteller.

Besides me, one of the people you would meet at the Center is my wife, Jean, who is a teacher. Vince Walsh is another old friend who used to climb trees with my brother, Jesse, when they were young. Today he is our expert tracker and wilderness guide. Paul Hetzler is a tree and plant specialist. There is also my Aunt Margaret, who is a storyteller.

Ndakinna is always growing. In the future we hope to offer scholarships to the center to children and young people from the city who have never had a chance to learn about nature. We also want to provide mentors or advisors for Native American young people. They will then be able to learn about the wilderness from the older people, just as my brother and I did from our father.

I tell stories, too.

With all these changes, one thing remains the same. As my grandmother wished, Ndakinna will always remain wild for future generations to enjoy.

Nature Notes

There are many programs kids can be a part of at the center. They include Wigwam Construction, Native American Games, Stalking Games, Native American Monster Stories, and Northeastern Native American History and Culture.

Glossary

appreciation [uh pree shee AY shun] the act of understanding, enjoying, and being grateful for

conservation [kahn sur VAY shun] the act of taking care of and protecting something, such as forests, water, and other natural resources

inspired [ihn SPYRD] caused or influenced to do something

intact [ihn TAKT] kept in one piece, or left whole, with nothing missing

mentors [MEN torz] teachers, coaches, or wise advisors

naturalist [NACH rul ihst] a person who studies nature, especially plants and animals

preserve [prih ZURV] as a noun, a place where something, such as wildlife, is protected; as a verb, to protect from harm or damage

respect [rih SPEKT] to feel or show honor for; think highly of; be thoughtful about

traditions [truh DIHSH unz] customs and beliefs handed down from generation to generation

variations [vayr ee AY shunz] changes from a basic form

48